North American EXPLORERS

By Yannick Oney

World Discovery History Reader™

SCHOLASTIC INC.

New York • Toronto • London • Auckland • Sydney
Mexico City • New Delhi • Hong Kong • Buenos Aires

North American Explorers

At one time, **North America** was a strange place. The lakes, rivers, and mountains of North America had not been mapped. The ocean stretching from Europe to the United States had not been crossed. Men and women who traveled to these faraway places were called **explorers**. Here are four stories of amazing explorers. Their travels helped shape America.

CHAPTER 1

Christopher Columbus, 1451–1506

Years of Exploration: 1492–1504

The sailors aboard the *Niña*, the *Pinta*, and the *Santa Maria* were scared. They did not see land. There was water as far as the eye could see. But there was no land. Maybe their captain was wrong. Maybe they would never see land again.

Christopher Columbus

Their captain was Christopher Columbus. He believed that they would find land soon. He believed that they were on their way to the islands near India. These islands were known in Columbus' time as the **Indies**.

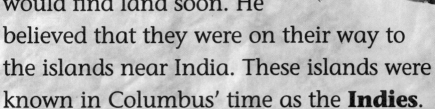

Columbus looked over the side of his ship. There was seaweed. The sailors lifted it onto the deck. They found a crab in the seaweed. Columbus knew it was a sign. "It means land is near!" he said.

More than two months earlier, Columbus and his men left Spain. Columbus thought he could find a faster way to get to the Indies. The Spanish King Ferdinand and Queen Isabella gave Columbus the money he needed for the trip. Columbus and his men left Spain on August 3, 1492.

Columbus, Queen Isabella, and King Ferdinand of Spain

Even though his crew was fearful, Columbus was confident that they would find land.

The weeks passed. The men had never been so far from home before. There was not much food left. The bread was green with mold. The barrels of freshwater were almost empty. The men wanted to turn the ships around and sail back to Spain. Columbus told the men not to worry. Land was near.

Columbus and his crew saw whales—creatures that no Spaniard had ever seen before.

7

On October 12, 1492, a sailor shouted, "Land, land!" The sailors landed on the shores of a strange place. They saw **native** people who called themselves **Tainos**. The Tainos wore brightly colored feathers in their hair. Some of them wore gold jewelry.

Map of the Atlantic Ocean drawn by Juan de la Cosa. He was Columbus' pilot and navigator. He also owned the *Santa Maria*.

Tainos greet Columbus and his landing party.

"These must be **Indians**," Columbus thought. "We have landed in the Indies!" But Columbus was wrong. He had landed on the **Caribbean** island that we now know as San Salvador in the **Bahama Islands**.

Columbus sailed to many of the different islands in the Caribbean. He was always looking for gold and riches. He made four trips back and forth from the islands to Spain.

Christopher Columbus died on May 20, 1506. He died believing he had found the Indies. Columbus never did find them. He found a whole new world instead.

Tainos bringing food and supplies to the explorers

Juan Ponce de León

CHAPTER 2

Juan Ponce de León, 1460–1521
Years of Exploration: 1493–1521

The natives in the Caribbean knew a good story. On an island called Bimini was a magical fountain. If you drank water from the fountain you would never grow old. The natives told this story to the Spaniards. The Spaniards ruled the Caribbean Islands.

Ponce de León was governor of a Caribbean island called **Borinquén**. Today this island is known as Puerto Rico. He ruled this island for the King of Spain. Ponce de León made the natives mine for gold.

Caribbean
Islands

In 1511, the King of Spain named a new governor to rule Borinquén. Ponce de León was out of a job. He remembered the story of the magical fountain of youth. Ponce de León wanted to find the magical fountain. A single cup of water from the fountain would be worth more than a ton of gold.

Spanish weapons and armor from the time of Columbus and Ponce de León

In 1513, Ponce de León set out to find the fountain of youth. It was Easter time. Ponce de León stood on his ship. He looked out across the ocean. In front of him he saw what looked like a large island.

Florida flamingo

In the Spanish language, Easter is called the "Passover of Flowers." Ponce de León decided to call the large island "la Florida." It means "the flowered one." Ponce de León did not know it, but he didn't land on an island. He landed on what we now know as Florida!

It is easy to see why Ponce de León thought Florida was an island!

Ponce de León still wanted to find the fountain of youth. He sailed south. One day something strange happened. His ships could not move forward. They were moving backward! It was not the wind. The wind was moving forward. But why was the ship moving backward?

The ship was sailing over a strong **current**. Ponce de León discovered what is known today as the **Gulf Stream**. It flows north for thousands of miles. It was an important discovery. The Gulf Stream helps many ships today travel north quickly. It is the fast lane of the **Atlantic Ocean**.

The Gulf Stream

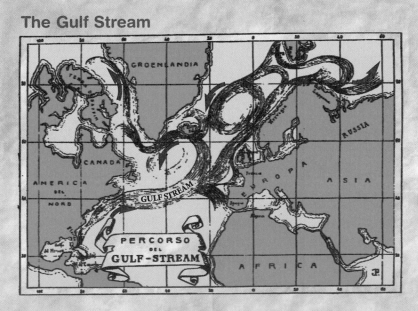

The Gulf Stream helped make Spain rich. The Gulf Stream was the fastest route for sailors to bring gold and riches from America to Spain. When Ponce de León landed in Florida, he was one of the first to discover what is now called the United States.

Ponce de León never did find the fountain of youth. His search for it led to some of the greatest discoveries of the **New World**.

Ponce de León and his party test the waters of a spring to see if it is the fountain of youth.

Lewis, Clark, and Sacagawea from "Lewis and Clark at Three Forks" by Edgar S. Paxson

CHAPTER 3

Meriwether Lewis, 1774–1809

William Clark, 1770–1838

Years of Exploration: 1804–1806

America had just bought land from the French. This purchase was called the **Louisiana Purchase**. America paid 15 million dollars for the land. This land covered an area more than 800,000 square miles (2 million square km). The land stretched west from the Mississippi River to the foot of the Rocky Mountains. Purchasing this land doubled the size of the United States.

Louisiana Purchase

President Thomas Jefferson wanted to know if a boat could travel by river all the way to the **Pacific Ocean**. From the Pacific Ocean, the United States could easily trade with Asia. He also wanted to know what the new territory was like. He wondered what the plants and animals were like. He wondered what the Native American tribes were like.

York and the Mandan tribe, from a painting by Charles Russell. The Mandans had never seen a person of African ancestry. They were fascinated by York's skin.

President Jefferson asked Captain Meriwether Lewis and Lewis's cocaptain, William Clark, to map the West. He also asked the explorers to send back samples of new plants and animals.

Lewis and Clark hired about forty men to go with them. In 1804, **slavery** was legal. Clark had an African slave named York. York also went with Lewis and Clark.

A pirogue—the flat-bottom boats that Lewis and Clark used to navigate the shallow Missouri

The party left Illinois on May 14, 1804. They began their journey by sailing on the Missouri River. The river was muddy and not very deep. The boats got stuck. For miles the men had to use ropes to pull their boats.

The Lewis and Clark expedition experienced many mornings like this on the Missouri River.

Winter came. The river froze. The men could not sail. They built a **fort** in North Dakota. They called it Fort Mandan. Lewis and Clark met a **Shoshone** Indian woman named Sacagawea. Her husband was a trapper named Toussaint Charbonneau. That winter she had a baby boy. The baby was named Jean Baptiste Charbonneau. Captain Clark nicknamed him "Pompey."

Re-creation of Fort Mandan in North Dakota

Sacagawea said she would help Lewis and Clark. The Shoshone **tribe** lived near the **Rocky Mountains**. She would talk to the Shoshone in her language. She would ask them for horses the men would need for the trip. That spring, Sacagawea and her family sailed west with Lewis and Clark.

Sacagawea and Charbonneau were very helpful to the expedition. Sacagawea spoke both Shoshone and Hidatsa Indian languages. She helped Lewis and Clark speak with native people they met on their journey. Because of her, the expedition was less likely to be attacked by warring native tribes. After all, a woman was traveling with the expedition—a woman with her infant boy strapped to her back.

"Sacajawea Guiding the Lewis and Clark Expedition"
by Alfred Russell

The water in the Missouri River was
rough. One time Charbonneau lost control
of his boat. Many of Lewis's and Clark's
belongings fell into the river. Sacagawea
moved fast. She saved their journals and
other important supplies.

These pages from Clark's journals show a candlefish and a sage grouse. Lewis and Clark described 122 animals (including the coyote, prairie dog, and porcupine) and 178 plants, all new to science.

When the **expedition** met the Shoshone tribe, Sacagawea was happy to see her people again. Sacagawea was able to get Lewis and Clark the horses they would need for their journey.

The trail up the Rocky Mountains was steep. The worst part was the Lolo Trail near the present-day **border** between Idaho and Montana. The trail was cold and icy. **Moccasins** turned into blocks of ice. The horses slipped time and time again. There was nothing to eat. The explorers were sick and starving.

The explorers came to the Columbia River. It flowed west. The men made **canoes** and set sail again. On November 7, 1805, the explorers came to an amazing sight. It was the Pacific Ocean!

Indian Graves Lookout on the Lolo Trail in Idaho

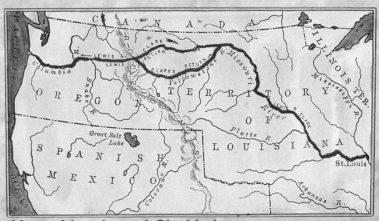

Map of Lewis and Clark's journey

On March 23, 1806, the explorers began their long journey home. When they finally returned back East, people were surprised to see them. More than two years had passed since they began their journey. Everyone thought they had died.

Lewis and Clark became American **heroes**. Americans learned it was not possible to travel all the way by boat to the Pacific Ocean. Americans learned there was good land to grow **crops**. There were plenty of animals to hunt. People could live there. Lewis and Clark gave their maps and journals to President Jefferson. The West was no longer a mysterious place.

Matthew Henson
and Robert Peary

CHAPTER 4

Matthew Henson, 1866–1955
Robert E. Peary, 1856–1920
Years of Exploration: 1891–1909

Crack! Crack! went the whip. **Husky dogs** pulled Matthew Henson's **sledge** over the polar ice cap toward the **North Pole**. Henson's **Inuit** friends had taught him how to drive the sledge dogs. When the Inuits first met Henson, they thought he, too, was an Inuit. Henson was an African American. His skin was dark like theirs.

Sledge used in the Henson/Peary expedition to the North Pole

The ice on the trail was bumpy. Henson's sledge broke. He took off his bearskin mittens to fix it. Every few seconds he had to stop. He had to put his hands under his reindeer fur jacket to keep warm.

Will we make it this time? thought Henson. The year was 1909. It was Matthew Henson and Robert E. Peary's third try to reach the North Pole. All the people in the expedition were worried. Would they reach the North Pole before the weather stopped them?

Matthew Henson

This Inuit doll shows the fur clothing that North Pole explorers might have worn.

Beneath Henson and Peary, the ice creaked and groaned. The men came to a wide stream of ocean water. It

Inuit boots

was not frozen. The explorers could not cross it until it was frozen. Would they have to turn back again?

Finally, the temperature dropped. It was now nearly -50° Fahrenheit (-46° Celsius). The water was frozen hard. At last the explorers could continue their journey to the Pole.

Seal meat has a high amount of vitamin C. Henson knew he had to eat fresh seal meat so that he wouldn't get scurvy. Scurvy is a disease caused by too little vitamin C.

It took Inuits only an hour to build an igloo. They used fifty to sixty blocks of snow. Each block was 6" x 18" x 24". The blocks were stacked in a spiral, closing in on the center.

Peary's party traveled more than twenty-four miles a day. When it was time to sleep, the men built **igloos** out of the ice. They slept on polar bear fur mats placed on the floor. Strips of fur tied around the men's eyes helped keep out the light so they could sleep. In the summer, the **Arctic** sun never sets.

The explorers kept moving to the Pole. They had only 135 miles to go! Henson came to a stream of water covered by thin ice. The ice broke and he fell in! One of Henson's Inuit friends pulled Henson out of the water. Henson's furs were soaked with icy water, but he was still alive. Henson got up and kept going.

The ice was smooth now. The sledges traveled fast. Three miles to go! They kept racing forward. Then they stopped. Had they reached the North Pole? Peary wanted to be sure. He went ahead without Henson to different points and checked his **sextant** to see where they were. They were going south! They had gone beyond the North Pole! They had to turn around and travel north again.

On April 6, 1909, Henson and Peary reached the North Pole. They had been searching for the North Pole for a long time. Their search for the North Pole was difficult. Storms were harsh. The men often ran out of food and had nothing to eat but their dogs. Peary lost eight toes to **frostbite**. And two men lost their lives. But Peary and Henson did it. They reached the top of the world!

Matthew Henson (center) holds the U.S. flag at the North Pole.

Glossary

Arctic: The area of land surrounding the North Pole.

Atlantic Ocean: The world's second largest ocean.

Bahama Islands: An Island country made up of over 700 islands off the Eastern coast of Florida.

Border: The line where an area begins and another ends.

Borinquén: Puerto Rico's original name.

Canoes: Light, narrow boats pointed at the ends and moved forward by paddles.

Caribbean: The entire area of the Caribbean Sea. It includes hundreds of islands that are between Florida in the North and Venezuela in the South.

Crops: Plants grown in fields.

Current: A path of water that is in motion.

Expedition: A group of people that makes a journey.

Explorers: People who travel to discover new places.

Fort: A protected area or building.

Frostbite: Injury or harm to part of the body, caused by being out in very cold temperatures.

Gulf Stream: A warm current in the North Atlantic Ocean that moves Northeast, then East.

Heroes: People who are known for their bravery, character, and/or special achievements.

Husky dogs: Dogs with thick, furry coats traditionally used for pulling sleds in the far North.

Igloos: A dome-shaped building made with blocks of ice or hard snow.

Indians: Name once used to describe native or original people of North and South America.

Indies: A group of islands in the Indian and Pacific Oceans between Asia and Australia.

Inuit: A member of the native people who live in the northernmost parts of North America.

Louisiana Purchase: 800,000 square miles of land that the United States bought from the French in 1803.

Moccasins: Soft leather slippers or shoes without a heel.

Native: A member in a group of people first known to have lived in a place.

New World: One of the names used for the continents of North and South America during the 16th century.

North America: The third largest continent. It includes the United States, Canada, and Mexico.

North Pole: The northernmost point of the world.

Pacific Ocean: The world's largest ocean.

Polar ice cap: A large section of ice at the top of the world.

Rocky Mountains: Major mountain system of North America that runs from New Mexico to Alaska.

San Salvador: One of the islands found in the Bahama Islands.

Sextant: A navigational tool that measures the distance between stars and other objects found in the visible sky.

Shoshone: A person who belongs to the Shoshone Native American tribe.

Slavery: The practice of owning people (slaves) so they can work without being paid money.

Sledge: A sled pulled by dogs.

Tainos: A group of people who lived in the various Caribbean islands such as Cuba, Jamaica, Hispaniola [Haiti and the Dominican Republic], and Puerto Rico.

Tribe: A group of people who share the same language, culture, and ancestry.